DREAMING
SMALL

INTIMATE
INTERIORS

DREAMING SMALL

INTIMATE INTERIORS

Douglas Woods

Photography by Melba Levick

RIZZOLI
NEW YORK

New York Paris London Milan

First published in the United States of America in 2014 by
RIZZOLI INTERNATIONAL PUBLICATIONS, INC.
300 Park Avenue South, New York, NY 10010
www.rizzoliusa.com

ISBN-13: 978-0-8478-4231-5
Library of Congress Control Number: 2013948343

Distributed to the U.S. Trade by Random House, New York

Front cover: Sitting room, Hobart House, Los Angeles (p. 116)
Back cover: (Clockwise from upper left) Howard–Nagin House (p. 162), Santa Monica Bungalow (p. 78),
Howard–Nagin House, Cavanagh Adobe (p. 48), Storybook Bohemian (p. 146), Spanish Bungalow (p. 86)
Endpapers: Storybook Bohemian

Page 2: Living room, Withers Residence, Beachwood Canyon, 1926 (p. 58)
Pages 6–7: Detail, Cavanagh Adobe, Indian Wells, 1922 (p. 48)

Designed by Douglas Curran

Printed and bound in China

2014 2015 2016 2017 2018 2019 / 10 9 8 7 6 5 4 3 2 1

CONTENTS

INTRODUCTION

LEFT *Detail of an art-filled alcove and bar. The plaster fish is by artist Jean-Pascal Flavien. Fraser House, Pasadena, 1928 (p. 68).*

FOR WELL OVER A CENTURY, people have been designing houses to suit the Southern California lifestyle. Big or small, the successful ones embrace the region's perpetually good weather and treat the garden as an equal in design. These houses are dreams realized and, in some cases, are also an imagined past made real. Los Angeles continues to attract people from all corners. Some are tugged by nostalgia, others are drawn by the chance to start afresh. Many continue to be pulled in by the opportunity to join the creative community, the thread that connects our collective conscience: Hollywood. The sum of all these parts defines the city's continuing allure.

But this book is about houses....

After the Great War, thousands of small houses sprung up across the Southland to accommodate the large migration of job seekers hoping for a slice of the West's booming prosperity. Many were designed for these new workers, but they hardly evoke "worker housing." Rather, they were often thoughtfully designed, scaled-down cousins of the grand revival-style houses being built in the foothills for the city's elite. The early penchant for Victorian architecture quickly gave way to the Arts and Crafts movement, which spawned thousands of charming bungalows inspired by the Greene, Heineman, and Stickley brothers. Later, through the 1920s, the venerable Spanish Colonial Revival style and influential early Modern movement thrived side by side and, in the case of genius architect Irving Gill, even combined strengths. Blocks and blocks of these mostly two-bedroom houses exhibited a particular regional flair and became an enduring image of the Los Angeles of postcards and booster ephemera.

A second, larger wave of building took off after the end of World War II and left the region with more single-family homes than any other city in America. This vast carpet of subdivisions gave midcentury Los Angeles its sprawling low profile and the feel of being a really big Midwest town, not the budding metropolis it is now becoming. Today, with the city all but completely built out, the trend is toward density and building higher. This, of course, is viewed as a threat to the city's now historic neighborhoods, whose residents have sprung into action over recent decades to create historic-preservation overlay zones to stop redevelopment wherever it can be justified. Viewed through this historical lens, it is easy to see why the rich legacy of Southern California's "everyday" houses is appreciated now more than ever.

A new generation has rediscovered these houses and is living in them better than ever. The jewel boxes celebrated in these pages champion an eclectic sense of style and a quality of life still uniquely Californian. Some are period-perfect time capsules while others are wildly reimagined re-creations. All are a testament to how these well-designed houses hold up in the twenty-first century.

RIGHT *Living room detail. Citrus House, Hancock Park 1925 (p. 106).*
FOLLOWING PAGES *Detail. Santa Monica Bungalow (p. 78).*

REPURPOSING THE PAST

SOUTHERN CALIFORNIA IS EVOLVING past the habit of cherry-picking facets of history to define itself. The region's historical roots are rich and deserve to be celebrated. With this in mind, many have been inspired to do quality artistic restorations of their old homes. A faithful restoration does not have to preclude one from incorporating today's technologies into an old house. The art lies in putting oneself in the shoes of the period home-owner and imaging what he or she would want in this day and age. A cowboy would appreciate a refrigerator and air-conditioning. The owner may opt to go beyond a restoration and turn the home into a showcase for his or her art. This lends not just to preservation but continues the evolution of the life of the home. The best old houses are really never done.

RIGHT *Tiled hood over an old Dutch door.*

BUNKHOUSE

FRENCH RANCH, HIDDEN VALLEY, 1922

"NO ONE LOVES SOUTHERN CALIFORNIA history more than a transplanted New Yorker." So says the man behind the meticulously executed ground-up restoration of this former bunkhouse in southern Ventura County.

Part of what was a 3,500-acre working ranch in the Conejo Valley, it was originally designed to house three rancheros. The board-and-batten American Prairie–style house has been converted into what the owner refers to as a "cheap and cheerful" single-family home filled with a combination of rare Monterey furniture and early to midcentury Americana. There are also items original to the house, such as the barrel-back chairs on the front porch. The back porch, screened-in to protect against wild animals and snakes, is actually an outdoor room where, without the luxury of air-conditioning, workers likely spent many summer nights in the warm valley.

In addition to a henhouse near the cottage, the property also has a neighboring stable house with three stalls for the horses and a saddle room and, in a bit of American folly, is crowned with an octagonal tower designed to house homing pigeons—a popular hobby in the 1920s.

The compound has the aura of a world now very much in our past but it also is a living testament to the hearty Midwesterners who helped build Southern California.

RIGHT *A 1950 Ford F1 pickup truck parked next to the old bunkhouse porch..*

PREVIOUS PAGES *A tractor-themed sprinkler sits atop an old ironing board in the living room.* ABOVE AND RIGHT *The kitchen and dining area.*

PREVIOUS PAGES *Monterey furniture in one of the bedrooms.*
LEFT *The stable house. The octagonal tower was designed to house homing pigeons.*
ABOVE *On the porch, barrel-back chairs original to the ranch.*

BUNGALOW AND TILE STUDIO

OJAI (date unknown)

THIS ONETIME WORLD WAR II–ERA U.S. Army barracks was originally situated at Point Hueneme in Ventura County. After the war, it was moved to its present site near downtown Ojai to be used as a bunkhouse for railroad workers. It remained a bunkhouse for many decades, gradually becoming dilapidated.

In 1994, the bunkhouse and land upon which it stood were bought by tile artisans Richard Keit and Mary Kennedy, who, seeing only "location, location, and a great stove," were undaunted by the task of restoring the old structure and transforming it and its surroundings into a wondrous showcase for their craft. Though the original footprint remains close to what it was, the house is unrecognizable from when they bought it.

Salvaged doors and windows were stripped and refinished, with any new glass replaced by older rippled glass. They added, as well, built-in bookcases by furniture makers Cyril and Sheila Wisneski and custom oak cabinetry by CD Builders of Thousand Oaks. The plaster walls were treated to eleven coats of beeswax and tons of elbow grease. A friend built the Arts and Crafts–style porch. The eaves were extended to thirty inches and sheathed in copper. Local stone now anchors the house and is thoughtfully placed throughout the landscaping.

The house is filled with an array of rosaries, santos, Van Briggle pottery, Japanese abacai, abalone shells and a variety of other antiques and curiosities. Inside and out, what really brings the house to life is the masterful tile work produced by their RTK Studios. Richly detailed murals animate the walls and floors. Decorative tiles bring the fireplace to life, and tile and mosaic pots accent the house.

RIGHT: *Tile and mosaic pots complement the porch's careful stonework.*

PREVIOUS PAGES *(Left) The beautifully tiled porch. (Right) Local produce on a Ries Niemi chair.*
ABOVE *A sunlit corner alcove.*
BELOW *A fireplace alcove surrounded by custom bookcases designed by Cyril & Sheila Wisneski.*
RIGHT *A bedroom.*

LEFT *This section of the house began as a dirt-floor garage.*
ABOVE AND BELOW *Outdoor living, Ojai style.*

33

ABOVE *RTK Studios, near studio.*
BELOW *Outdoor dining area.*
RIGHT *Mary Kennedy's workshop.*

RANCHO DULCE

OJAI, 1928

THIS HOUSE, BUILT IN 1928 among acres of citrus groves, started out as a single-story one-bedroom house with two fireplaces. Though likely designed without an architect, there was clearly an accomplished stone-mason on site. Built for a local schoolteacher, the house and gardens have evolved over time and now include a second-floor renovation, which enclosed the original outdoor sleeping porch to create what is now a studio.

Today, it is the country home of renowned landscape architect Pamela Burton and her husband, Richard Hertz, a historian of contemporary Los Angeles art. Their passion for the region stems from memories they share of growing up near citrus orchards. They tend around 1,000 Minneola tangelo, Valencia orange, and olive trees of their own. From her second-floor studio, Burton can survey the land that has informed and inspired her work. Over the years, she has added a network of native stone walls and, more recently, a swimming pool to the landscape.

The defining motifs of the home's interior are a worldly combination of books, contemporary art, Asian and Hispanic antiques, and great garden views.

RIGHT *Sylvan approach to Rancho Dulce.*

PREVIOUS PAGES *Above the fireplace in the family room, John Baldessari's* Prima Facie (Second State): Stone *adds twenty-first-century drama to the rustic retreat.* ABOVE AND RIGHT *The kitchen and dining areas.*

LEFT *From the bedroom windows, the view opens to a persimmon tree and the mountains beyond. Painting by James Hayward.* ABOVE *The enclosed sleeping porch is now used as Pamela Burton's work space. From the desk, expansive views of the groves beyond are visible.*
BELOW *The painting,* Pamela's Secrets, *by artist Jane Wells, is in honor of Burton's designs.*
FOLLOWING PAGES *A December view of the recently completed pool with baskets of Bearss limes and persimmons.*

THE SPANISH COLONIAL TRADITION TODAY

THE PANAMA–CALIFORNIA EXPOSITION of 1915 in San Diego ushered in a golden era of architectural design in Southern California. Organized to celebrate the completion of the Panama Canal, the expo's lasting impact was its kindling of the region's imagination of itself as a Spanish Revival fantasyland. Chief architect Bertram Grosvenor Goodhue, along with fellow architect Carleton Winslow, was responsible for its master plan, and the two designed many of the expo's noteworthy buildings. The still-standing buildings of Balboa Park, San Diego, where the expo was held, mark the birthplace of the architecture of our "new Spain" and today continue to serve as benchmark examples of the style. Though the important early modernist Irving Gill argued that the future park should reflect a more restrained blend of Mission and International styles, Goodhue's elaborate designs were what captured the public's imagination and won out. Different iterations of the casa evolved throughout Southern California in the 1920s and '30s, resulting in homes that combined everything a Hollywood set designer could conjure, from the authentic reproductions of John Byers and his studio to Robert Stacey-Judd's Mayan Deco creations. Along with Goodhue's own, the grandiose *castillos* of Julia Morgan and John DeLario took the style to its limits.

The integral elements of most casas are their courtyard or walled gardens. Hidden from the outside, these secret gardens provide privacy usually reserved for a home's interior and offer the opportunity to connect the rooms of the house to the garden. The courtyard design also lends itself well to multi-residence living, allowing private apartments clustered around a common walled garden and fountain and creating an instant community. Courtyard apartment buildings, like those pioneered by husband-and-wife architects

Arthur and Nina Zwebell, can be found all over Southern California. Grander examples of the Spanish Revival style contained multiple courtyards, patios, pergolas, and verandas. These elements afforded the experience of living as a Southern Californian should. Architect Cliff May was quoted to have said, "If you can't walk out of the living room or bedroom or kitchen onto the ground, if you have to go down steps, you're not living like a real Californian lives." Denizens of the southwest and Mexico would not have found this news, but May's point made it plain and clear for the uninitiated.

  The influence of these homes is wide-reaching. Gill's urging of the melding of the Mission and the Modern happened. It can be seen in his own work, and it inspired an understanding of how the European International style could be translated to Southern California's Mediterranean-like environment as evident in the work of Richard Neutra and other early Modern architects. In this case, glass and steel replaced adobe and iron, but it was still ultimately all about providing a house to ideally and economically suit most anyone striving to comfortably enjoy a part of Southern California's burgeoning indoor-outdoor lifestyle. The influence on imitators continues today, witnessed in the countless cookie-cutter suburban tracts that cheaply mimic Spanish and other Mediterranean-style details. Few builders in this style today match the level of quality and craftsmanship that those of the 1920s and '30s achieved. Architects such as George Washington Smith and Wallace Neff took these time-tested perfect houses to their apex in proportion and lines.

  While the history conjured up by the Spanish Revival style is more imagined than real, it continues to define the ideal of Southern California for many.

CAVANAGH ADOBE

INDIAN WELLS, 1922
H. ANDERSON SANDERS, ARCHITECT

THIS ADOBE HOUSE, BEGUN in 1922 and constructed over the following several years, was the home of early Palm Desert residents, brothers Albert and Hubert Cavanagh and is possibly the oldest standing structure in the region. Hubert "Bert" Cavanagh was instrumental in developing the area and came up with the name that the city goes by today, Indian Wells.

Constructed with thousands of four-inch-by-twelve-inch-by-eighteen-inch bricks handmade by Mexican workers, the rectangular house, with its massive fireplace, was once surrounded by twenty acres of citrus and dates. Its clay roof tiles, handmade by a La Quinta resident named Joe Valenzuela, bear a distinctive shape, made by bending clay over one's thigh. These hearty handmade tiles hold up still today. Originally two bedrooms, one bath, and a second-story sleeping porch, the house has been thoroughly restored by husband-and-wife architects Michael Burch and Diane Wilk. It is a significant remaining link to the area's historic date industry, which, with less than twenty palms of the original twenty acres of trees remaining today, has all but disappeared.

RIGHT *Painted Monterey furniture is gathered around the fireplace.*

ABOVE AND RIGHT *A sitting nook and a view of the living room.*

LEFT *The dining room.*

ABOVE *The original shutters, with cut out date-palm flourishes.*
RIGHT *The thickly painted adobe brick facade.*
FOLLOWING PAGES *The dining patio.*

WITHERS RESIDENCE

BEACHWOOD CANYON, 1926
L. A. SMITH, ARCHITECT

LOCATED AT THE FOOT of Mount Lee, known worldwide for its famed Hollywood sign, this house is one of the original five built as part of the Hollywoodland development. Of course, the sign no longer reads *Hollywoodland*, and the surrounding hills have now been overbuilt with structures. Still, this enclave at the mouth of Beachwood Canyon does not feel dense and has a quiet, sequestered feel to it, even though it isn't much more than a stone's throw from the city's bustle. Designed by architect L. A. Smith, this one-story Spanish-style house is the kind oft emulated at the time, with its high-beamed ceiling and courtyard fountain clad in Malibu tile, and is a historic cultural monument.

This house proves yet again that these simple white stucco Mediterraneans are great for showcasing art. The owners, David Pagel and Alisa Tager, along with decorator Carol Vena-Mondt (who designed most of the furniture in the living room), achieved a pleasing balance in merging vibrant contemporary art with old-world details.

RIGHT *A street view of the house, one of the original Hollywoodland homes.* FOLLOWING PAGES *A corner of the art-filled living room with a painting by Nancy Mitchnick (at left) and Polly Apfelbaum's* Flags of Revolt and Defiance. PAGES 62–63 *(Left) Netter pottery over the fireplace with a digital print by Nicholas Shake. (Right) On the coffee table, 1960s resin candle holders by Sascha Brastoff. Other paintings in the living room are by Ian Trout, John Mills and Andrew Ballstaedt.*

LEFT *The dining room.*
ABOVE *Children's room.*
BELOW *Bedroom.*
FOLLOWING PAGES *The courtyard garden with Malibu-tile fountain.*

FRASER HOUSE

PASADENA, 1928
FITCH HASKELL, ARCHITECT

PASADENA HAS NO SHORTAGE of great houses. Block after block of well maintained, grand period-revival-style homes line her streets, and many landmarks call this city home, including the Arts and Crafts treasure, the Gamble House by Charles and Henry Greene, and Frank Lloyd Wright's La Miniatura. The Spanish Revival is well represented here, including works by the architect George Washington Smith as well as mansions designed by Wallace Neff.

This picturesque Spanish Colonial Revival house, situated among a canopy of oak and olive trees, shares the hallmarks of its larger neighbors, including thick stuccoed walls punctuated by sweeping arches, decorative ironwork, hardware, and tile, and, though smaller in scale, feels grand thanks to the voluminous proportions of the public rooms. Attributed to architect Fitch Haskell, the house, despite its relatively modest footprint, has the noble presence of some of Haskells renowned buildings, such as the Pasadena Civic Auditorium and All Saints' Church.

Today, the house is home to acclaimed artist John Millei and his family. The generous walls of the house and studio (converted from the garage) prove a perfect setting to display his large expressionistic canvases.

RIGHT *From the approach, the house presents an elegant countenance with thick stucco walls, iron grilles, and a red tiled roof, all elements of a classic Spanish Revival house.*
FOLLOWING PAGES *View from the dining room looking toward the living room.*

ABOVE *View from kitchen.*
BELOW *Kitchen.*
RIGHT *The living room with Millei's* Woman in a Chair.

LEFT *The artist's watercolor studio in the enclosed porch.*
ABOVE *The children's bedroom.*
BELOW *The outdoor dining area.*

ECHOES OF MEXICO

THE HISTORIC RELATIONSHIP BETWEEN California and Mexico has provided a natural affinity for those seeking to have a piece of that past represented in their home.

The Mexican decorative arts should not be defined by the straw painted souvenirs of tourist beach resorts. A result of the European and indigenous confluence, the tradition of Mexican metalwork, pottery, tile, and other forms of *artesanía*, or, folk art, has drawn a devoted class of collectors. Also popular are the religious expressions of *milagros*, retablos, santos, tin crosses, and various faux reliquaries related to the celebration of *Dia de los Muertos*. This trend took off after the first major exhibition of its kind in Los Angeles in 1921 and continues to this day.

RIGHT *Detail from a Santa Monica bungalow with a portrait of Will Rogers in the background.*

SANTA MONICA BUNGALOW

SANTA MONICA, 1912

THIS 1912 HOUSE STARTED out a shingle-clad bungalow but was subsequently stuccoed over, which the current owners learned after seeing a set of photographs taken of the house in the 1920s. Inspired by what they saw, they took it upon themselves to restore the house to its original design—and then some. They stripped and refinished the shingles and replaced louvered windows with more appropriate Craftsman-style ones. They also replicated the original brick-and-river-rock pillars and curved steps leading up to the porch. Thankfully, the original built-in cabinets, stained glass and light fixtures survived. The house is now a showcase for the owners' extensive collection of Mexican wares.

RIGHT *Paintings mounted on shingles in the enclosed porch.*
FOLLOWING PAGES *The living room and dining room combine Craftsman-style furniture and an eclectic collection of crafts.*

ABOVE *Original built-in breakfront bookcase and foldout writing table.*
RIGHT *Living room corner with colorful textiles against original Craftsman-style paneling.*

LEFT *In the kitchen, original built-in cabinets surround a great antique Wedgewood stove.*
ABOVE *Breakfast nook detail.*
BELOW *The dining room.*

SPANISH BUNGALOW

RANCHO PARK, 1935

THIS HOUSE IS A GOOD example of the Spanish-style bungalows built across Los Angeles in the early part of the century. Though the ones built in the 1920s tended to have more expensive details than ones built after the crash of '29, the current owners of this once simpler 1935 house have done it the justice it deserves. Working with architect Anne Marie Madla, the owners raised the living room ceiling and dramatic beams added. As they put it, "We did a lot with a little." The landscaping was transformed from what was a surround of expansive lawn to a drought-tolerant landscape not unlike what one would find growing naturally in the desert regions.

RIGHT *A Spanish-style bungalow peeks out from behind a rescued garden of* Agave americana, Senecio mandraliscae, *and other California natives.*
FOLLOWING PAGES *The living room with period replica Batchelder fire surround and iron sconces produced by Ray Ferra.*

LEFT *Eat-in kitchen with Tlaquepaque collection on full display.*
ABOVE *"Everyday" dishware, both Bauer and Fiestaware. Colorful and stackable.*
BELOW *The dining room.*

ABOVE *In front of the Mexican tin tray, this painted lampshade evokes the spirit of the Old West.*
RIGHT *The guest room furnished with Coronado and Monterey furniture upholstered in vintage serapes.*

SPANISH TRANSFORMATION

SANTA MONICA, 1938

THOUGH IT APPEARS THAT this house always looked this way, it was actually a small redwood-sided bungalow when first built in 1938. The current owners, she a landscape architect and he a craftsman originally from Mexico, however, dreamed of a casa to complement their flea market collection of all things California and Mexico. Off went the siding, replaced with a traditional stucco finish, on went a red tile roof as well as abundant tile work. Today, it resembles a Mexican hacienda inside and out. Everything from its stone walls inspired by the ones found in Cuernavaca to the home's interior color pallette has an air of authenticity and truly does justice to their collection.

RIGHT *This hacienda-style bungalow is shaded by a massive* Eucalyptus cornuta. FOLLOWING PAGES *The living room replete with* crucifixos *and other religious art from Mexico.*

RIGHT *The dining area with a hand-built fireplace trimmed in talavera tile.*

LEFT *The tile-bedecked kitchen is at once supremely functional and festive.*
ABOVE *Bauer, Fiesta and Mexican pottery are displayed in a hutch among serapes and* saltillo.
BELOW *Blue and white chickens resting on blue and white talavera tile.*

ABOVE *Old painted gates brought from Mexico have been reintroduced here, under a planted tiled entry roof.*
RIGHT *Turtle pond.*

THE CALIFORNIA
BUNGALOW REIMAGINED

THE POSTWAR BUILDING BOOM of the 1920s gave Southern California thousands of small bungalows that have shown true staying power. Not a far throw from the Bengali bungalow of the British Raj, these interpretations, designed in a variety of period revival styles, were both a sober reaction to the Victorian era's penchant for wild ornament and a practical response to the needs of the more than one million migrants to the Golden State during this time. The bungalow phenomenon was fueled in part by the designs of Gustav Stickley in *The Craftsman* as well as by the plan books of Henry "The Bungalow Man" Wilson, The E. W. Stillwell Company, and Alfred and Arthur Heineman, all entrepreneurial designers that propagated the style nationwide. More than four walls and a roof to shelter from the elements, these bungalows were attainable homes with charm and dignity that made for a quality of domestic life the typical small-home owner was not used to at the time.

Much has been published on bungalow purity, and for good reason. The Arts and Crafts movement was all-encompassing, a uniform style of design that extended to every aspect of craft. Designed with both form and function in mind, the glasswork, ironwork, ceramics, tile, and furniture all worked in tandem to complement the architecture. The examples in this book, however, are not house museums. These once simple houses, through the artistic drive of their current owners, have evolved and now demonstrate unique personalities of their own.

RIGHT *Colorful turret entry in an Echo Park storybook bungalow.*

CITRUS HOUSE

HANCOCK PARK, 1925

THIS 1925 BUNGALOW WAS in a major state of disrepair when fashion designer and interior decorator Johnson Hartig first laid eyes on it, but he saw past the low ceilings and uneven floors, realizing all the hidden potential it possessed. He blew out the ceilings, redid the floors, lost the half-hearted Mediterranean details, painted everything white and filled the house with his signature mix of eye-popping art and old-world antiques. In the back, he built a totally private garden oasis, complete with a pool and decorated with hanging driftwood sculptures he created. Today, the wild, overgrown garden on the street side hides the surprise one is greeted by upon crossing the threshold into Hartig's world.

RIGHT *The private enclosed pool garden at the back of the house.*
FOLLOWING PAGES *The living room is chock-full of art and curiosities spanning centuries, including grotto chairs and an impressive Damien Hirst spin painting.*

RIGHT *The sitting room is full of treasures, including an Yves Saint Laurent Love pillow, a collection of Staffordshire dogs, and a portrait of Hartig in front of the bookcases, photographed for French* Vogue *by Andrew Durham.*

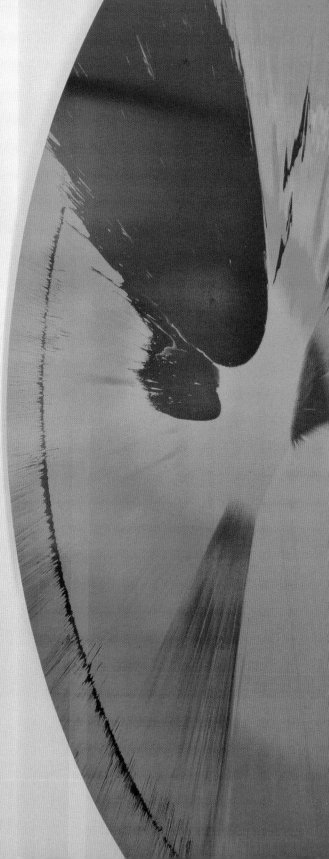

LEFT *Peeking into the kitchen past another Hirst spin painting.*
ABOVE *A glimpse of Hartig's collection of antique naval dioramas.*

113

ABOVE *A butterfly painting and* Knife through the Heart *by Damien Hirst.*
BELOW *Hartig's home workspace.*
RIGHT *In the master bedroom, a headboard with French hand-painted Zuber wallpaper.*

HOBART HOUSE

LOS ANGELES, 1911

THIS 1911 CRAFTSMAN IN the center of Los Angeles has the classic Arts and Crafts facade with its clinker-brick columns and chimney. The current owners, music supervisor Margaret Yen and her husband, artist Eric Ernest Johnson, wanted a completely different vibe for the interior of the house. First came a big remodel that involved blowing out walls and closets to expand the kitchen and open it up to the dining room. Thankfully, all the original hardware, andirons and built-in cabinetry remained, but new windows had to be installed, and the brickwork had to be restored.

With the help of friend and designer Johnson Hartig, they achieved a bright and airy interior that feels like an inviting 1970s beach cottage filled with art and fun.

RIGHT *A vintage Velzy surfboard from La Jolla on the back porch.* FOLLOWING PAGES *A quintessential early-twentieth-century bungalow; note the restored clinker-brick columns.*

PREVIOUS PAGES *In the living room, vintage Drexel furniture is at home with paintings by Eric Ernest Johnson and prints and sculptures by Niki de Saint Phalle.*
LEFT AND ABOVE *The expanded kitchen and dining room.*

ABOVE AND BELOW *The two bedrooms.*
RIGHT *The den featuring a wall covered in E. E. Johnson's paintings conceived by Johnson Hartig, who consulted on the interior design of the whole house.*

LEFT AND ABOVE *The Rogue's Retreat, a former garage turned into E. E. Johnson's home studio.*

WONDERLAND HOUSE

LOOKOUT MOUNTAIN, 1934

LOCATED IN A NEIGHBORHOOD steeped in music and Hollywood lore and not far from the intriguing Lookout Mountain Air Force Station—a secret studio set up during World War II to provide production services for classified military footage—this house is fittingly home to a family of creative types. Musicians, artists, and writers Bryan Ray Turcotte and his wife, Dayna, are raising their two boys in a house chock-full of family heirlooms and art that reflects the living legacy of the area. The house was built for a costume designer, sold to the current owners by a well-known actress, and today hosts jam sessions by the next generation of rockers and their friends.

RIGHT *The house presents a traditional facade tucked into the hillside.* FOLLOWING PAGES *In the living room, a large portrait by Aaron White and photographs by Dan Monick. On the coffee table in front of the stairs sits the original mold for the DEVO Energy Dome.*

LEFT *In the dining area, an early-nineteenth-century Irish pub table and Raymond Pettibon's* Use the Moon.
ABOVE *Family heirlooms around the mantel.*
BELOW *A Phil Frost painting leans against a wall near a table covered by modern Lucite-and-glass sculptures from Italy.*

ABOVE AND BELOW *Details of the boys' room.*
RIGHT *Looking past Evan Mack's* Lemon Head *to the bedroom,
complete with* Crass *pillowcases by James Rockin.*

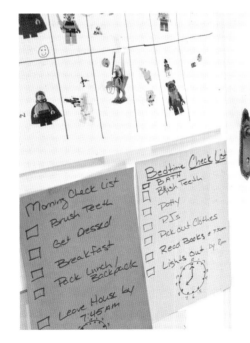

ROYAL COURT BUNGALOW

LOS ANGELES, 1921

THE OWNERS OF THIS simple 1921 bungalow south of Hancock Park found a unique north-facing site with a view of the Hollywood Hills and a challenge in working a family of four with too many books into a 1,400-square-foot space. Bliss was achieved, and the most was made of the view. With three bedrooms and two bathrooms cleverly laid out in the back third of the house, room was spared for a large eat-in kitchen, proper dining room, a small office, and a comfortable living room. The chimney was crumbling, but rather than replace it, they tore it down and installed a picture window over the mantel that now frames the hood ornament of Los Angeles, the famed Griffith Observatory by architects John C. Austin and Frederick M. Ashley. Bookcases were installed everywhere possible, though the volumes still continue to pile up.

RIGHT *On the porch, a Lutyens bench sits next to the typical California Craftsman door.*
FOLLOWING PAGES *From the living room past the bar and into the dining room, the decor is defined by books and heirloom antiques.*

LEFT *A closet was blown out to make a home office. Three generations of the family have learned to type on the antique Underwood typewriter to the right. Above it,* 5th Avenue in the Rain, *by Walter Yust.*

ABOVE *The book-filled dining room.* BELOW *The breakfast nook, with photographic elevations of New Orleans, Paris, and Venice, by Larry Yust.* RIGHT *Detail of the owners' collection of miniature books produced by Bela and Mariana Blau among other family treasures.*

RIGHT *In the bedroom, a rotating gallery.*

STORYBOOK BOHEMIAN

ECHO PARK, 1929

—— THIS 1929 STORYBOOK-STYLE house in the hills of Echo Park serves both as a studio and repository for artist Caitlin Wylde's obsessions and inspirations. The sperm-whale weather vane crowning the home's spire is a nod to Wylde's native Hartford, Connecticut, as is the collection of nautical and beach curiosities found throughout the house.

When the Wylde bought the house, its layout needed to be reconfigured. Undaunted, she accepted the challenge. The kitchen, needing expansion, found its way into the garage, and an interior staircase was added to access the downstairs portion of the house. Before the stairs, one had to go outside and walk down a sloping hill to access the rooms below. Today, the home is a marvel of spacial efficiency commingled with a bohemian, artistic spirit.

RIGHT *A sperm-whale weather vane caps the turret of this storybook bungalow.*

LEFT *Artist Caitlin Wylde's living room, with its sculpted-arch ceiling, features a fabric inspired by Matisse vestments and one of many beach-themed curio boxes found throughout the house.*
BELOW *A view of the colorful foyer.*

PREVIOUS PAGES *Living room detail with an antique decoy mounted on the wall and a Max Gottschalk chair.*
ABOVE *A Hungarian apothecary case full of beach treasures and art.*
RIGHT *Detail featuring an old Union 76 canvas advertisement.*

武町
前田
面

古消波商

NORTH AMERICAN FISH

PREVIOUS PAGES *A bedroom worked into the attic full of textiles, flea market prints, and a portrait of a family ancestor.*
LEFT *Wylde's art studio.*
FOLLOWING PAGES *Antique finds on the balcony overlooking Echo Park.*

STYLE TO SCALE,
BETWEEN THE WARS

BY THE 1930S, THE Spanish Colonial Revival style was so prevalent that it came to be considered common. Perhaps this was why those seeking to build in a period revival style began looking toward other parts of Europe for inspiration. This was also an era of downsizing for many.

As the nation segued into the Depression era, everyone learned to do more with less. While industrialists and celebrities were still commissioning grand-scale projects, their architects were also busy designing high-quality, modest-scale houses in such tony locations as Beverly Hills, Hancock Park, and Pasadena. Their other budget-wise clients saw the value of building a smaller, high-quality home over a low-quality big one. It's also worth noting that in those days, even the average spec home was better built than many are now, this being the era of able craftsmen and two-by-fours that actually measured two inches by four. Observing the quality craftsmanship of some of these houses today makes it hard to imagine them as any kind of compromise.

Stylish apartment buildings built in the French Norman, Art Deco, and other combined regional styles also went up around fashionable neighborhoods offering an alternative to those who wished to live by a golf course but couldn't necessarily afford a big house.

These golden age apartments were a slice of luxury living the rest of mostly suburban Los Angeles lacked. A big part of their appeal was their proximity to Wilshire Boulevard, then the Champs-Élysées of the West Coast and home to the Ambassador Hotel, Bullocks Wilshire, and I. Magnin. In contrast to today's typical cheap cookie-cutter apartment buildings, these structures are coveted for their spacious layouts and period details. They truly don't build them like this anymore.

HOWARD–NAGIN HOUSE

LOS ANGELES, 1929
PAUL R. WILLIAMS, ARCHITECT

BUILT IN 1929 AND declared a historic-cultural monument in 1989, this house, designed by architect Paul R. Williams in the Miracle Mile section of Los Angeles, is smaller than those often associated with him, but Williams's acute attention to detail is just as evident here as in any of the larger homes he designed.

Beautifully restored by the current owners with the help of Martin Eli Weil, one of the founders of the Los Angeles Conservancy, the house shares many features similar to those found in Williams's larger works. The living room has a grand-scale, double-height ceiling and opens up to a formal dining room. Plaster ceiling ribs in the breakfast nook and a dentil detail at the edge of the ceiling that continues in front of the bay window at the end of the room demonstrate an attention to detail without flaunting such care. As Williams always designed with outdoor entertaining in mind, the main rooms extend out to a covered porch that continues to the garden. Although the house had only two bedrooms upstairs originally, the second family made room for two boys by repurposing the attic space above the front door where Williams hid cabinets and drawers behind existing paneling.

RIGHT Partially obscured by the golden leaves of a Gingko tree, this scaled down Paul R. Williams English Tudor–style house has all the presence of the large houses for which he is well known.
FOLLOWING PAGES The grand scale living room opens out to the patio, as does the adjacent dining room, bringing the out-doors into the home.

ABOVE *Sun cast through the round stained glass window, probably by The Judson Studios of Highland Park.*
RIGHT *The wood-paneled dining room.*

LEFT *The decorative plastered ceiling in the breakfast nook is reminiscent of a detail Williams often used in his grander homes.*
RIGHT *The antique telephone is still in working order.*
FOLLOWING PAGES *To accommodate children, the attic space above the front door was ingeniously converted into quarters for two, with closet space worked in behind the paneling.*

FRENCH NORMAN TOWNHOUSE

WINDSOR VILLAGE, 1936

THIS NORMAN-STYLE BUILDING near Wilshire Boulevard has changed little since the 1930s and is a good example of courtyard apartment design. Buildings like these are popular not just for their character and details but also for the fact that the units share a garden instead of a hallway. Courtyard housing is most commonly associated with the Spanish- and Mexican-style structures developed by Arthur and Nina Zwebell in the early 1920s, but as these buildings proliferated, they were translated into a variety of architectural styles.

The residents of this stylish townhouse, writer David Wills and his partner, jewelry designer Jeffrey McCall, have created a hip blend of classic sixties photography, African art, and comfortable furniture.

RIGHT *The Rosenkranz Apartments, designed by Louis Selden in 1936, are an example of well-planned beautiful courtyard housing developed in 1930s Southern California.*

LEFT *In the living room, two Richard Avedon portraits of Faye Dunaway, as seen in the film* The Thomas Crown Affair, *on either side of the decorative mantel. The painting is a thrift-store find.*

175

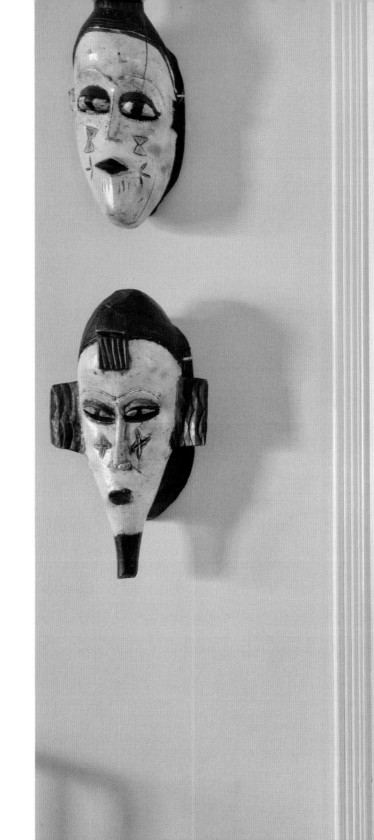

TOP *Living room detail.*
ABOVE *The master bedroom.*
RIGHT *Looking into the dining room, past late-nineteenth-century Fang tribe
masks to an Andre de Dienes portrait of Marilyn Monroe.*
FOLLOWING PAGES *A view of the courtyard from the balcony.*

MODERNE APARTMENT

WINDSOR VILLAGE, 1936

THIS BUILDING HAS BOTH Moderne and storybook qualities that combine to evoke a transitioning pre–World War II Europe. Its spacious and airy apartments, with high ceilings and generous layouts, provide the opportunity to make a proper apartment home.

This light-filled apartment of bicycle blogger and art prepareter Alex Yust and his wife, lighting designer Sandrine Junod, is one such home. Filled with Modern furniture, contemporary art, kid's stuff, and bicycles, the apartment still feels sparse and navigable.

RIGHT *A tall curved wall of windows fills the living room with light.*
FOLLOWING PAGES *Some classic Breuer and Le Corbusier furniture in the living room.*

COFFEE
MILK
HEROIN
CAT FOOD
BREAD

LOUIS
XXX

STREETS TELL STORIES 1
Photography by Larry Yust

STREETS TELL STORIES 2
Photography by Larry Yust

ANDY WARHOL

Andrew Zuckerman

On the books stacked on the table:

PUNK IS DEAD PUNK IS EVERYTHING

SHIGERU BAN

Frank Lloyd Wright's Price Tower

A SEAL OF ZEBRAS

FILMS

Architecture · Sculpture

BALDESSARI

Saul Bass

ABOVE *The kitchen.*
RIGHT *Wherever room can be found for bikes, it is put to good use—even in the dining room.*
FOLLOWING PAGES *The entry landing with Larry Yust's* Parliament.

Modernism Then and Now

THE EPIC RISE OF the early Modern movement fueled by Eastern European–born immigrant architects, notably Richard Neutra and Rudolf Schindler, gave birth to a style that, though rooted in the International Style, became synonymous with Los Angeles. Arriving at the perfect time and place to experiment, these early Modern architects took advantage of new building materials and technologies to pursue a sleek and ultimately affordable style of design that resonated with progressive-minded clients. Economizing space wherever possible was for many as much an economic necessity as it was a modernist ideal, and such architects became expert at paring things down to their essential functions while maintaining an elegance that taught people to see the beauty in industrial design. Their ideals, similar to their Arts and Crafts counterparts, were social-minded. Both strived to make architecture that was accessible and which offered solutions to societal challenges. The ripples this work created were felt late into the middle part of the twentieth century and inspired the work of later Modern architects, particularly those associated with Arts & Architecture editor, John Entenza's Case Study House Program, which lasted into 1960.

The Mediterranean-inspired tradition whereby the garden is treated as an extension of the house, so much a part of Southern California life by this time, influenced these architects as well. The climate here was such that the outdoors was always considered an element to be incorporated, whether through the use of courtyards as outdoor rooms or glass walls as a means to blur the line between inside and out and bring in light to all corners of the home.

NATURAL MODERN

LOS FELIZ, 1952

THIS 1952 LOS FELIZ HOUSE features a stylish pairing of Zen and Modern. A midcentury house with exposed beams, the home has a calming, naturalistic quality. The tea room in the front features a variety of wood furniture, including pieces from a Japanese estate as well as uniquely shaped George Nelson hanging lamps. Custom shelving designed by Amy Devers holds an extensive library of books and a 10,000-plus vinyl record collection. In lieu of curtains or shades, the owners opted for live bamboo, which provides a natural wall of privacy while still letting light through. The collection of art, ceramics, and pottery is primarily composed of pieces designed in Southern California during the middle part of the twentieth century. To add levity to the interiors, oddball and one-of-a-kind items found in thrift stores have been placed throughout the house.

RIGHT *Detail from the owner's extensive pottery collection.*
FOLLOWING PAGES *The tea room at the front of the house incorporates several varieties of wood furniture to enhance the feeling of nature. The George Nelson lamps add a midcentury touch.*

ABOVE, BELOW, AND RIGHT *The living room, warmed by exposed beams, houses an eclectic collection of furnishings, vinyl, and books. Over the fireplace is a 1957 serigraph by Los Angeles artist Richard Rubins.*

LEFT *A spare bedroom was converted into a media room and bar.*

ABOVE *The master bedroom.*

FOLLOWING PAGES *The hillside backyard is tiered on three levels, providing several privatized areas for contemplation. Citrus, yucca, bamboo, and avocado trees mix with lavender, rosemary, and succulents to create visual density and diversity.*

OHARA HOUSE

SILVER LAKE, 1959
RICHARD NEUTRA, ARCHITECT

FACING SILVER LAKE, THIS house steps down its sloped lot in four stages, maximizing possible floor space in a subtle and unexpected way. Though only about 1,400 square feet, the house has various areas that create the sense that it is bigger than it is. So absorbed in its site, the house embodies an ideal Neutra "machine in the garden."

Completed late in his career, it is a refined work. Now home to designer and writer David Netto and his family, the house is filled with a quality collection of art and furniture and a quality collection of children's art. The decor is not that of a Modern purist but rather goes against the grain of what one might expect in a house of this kind. The resulting interior is an expertly balanced and comfortable blend of new and old, Continental and Californian, and it all seems right at home in the glass-and-steel shell.

RIGHT *The dramatic stepped front facade.*

ABOVE *The rear entrance from the carport.*
RIGHT *The fountain was added by C. J. Bonura.*

LEFT *The careful mix of classic Modern and African furniture and Modern art against transparent walls recalls the de Menil House in Houston decorated by Charles James.*

FOLLOWING PAGES *A wider view of the living room, beautifully arranged by decorator Paul Fortune. On the T. H. Robsjohn-Gibbings table sits Jean Arp's Torse. Other pieces include a Poul Kjaerholm PK22 chair and Viennese barrel chairs from the 1920s.*

LEFT *A child's room.*
ABOVE *The master bedroom includes a Louis XV writing table and a television mounted on a reproduction Dupre-Lafon easel. The wall was decisively painted red to go with the tartan rug.*
BELOW *Children's art along with the work of artists Fontana and Twombly.*

BECKMAN RESIDENCE

HANCOCK PARK, 1938
GREGORY AIN, ARCHITECT

NESTLED AMONG A MIX of early-twentieth-century European revival style houses, this stunning interpretation of the International Style is a stand-out. The sleek but understated facade belies the gem that unfolds beyond the signature Ain arcade and through the front door.

The house had suffered years of neglect before its savior, Brooke Anderson, bought it. Inspired by childhood memories of growing up in a Modern 1950s home designed by Sumner Spaulding and John Rex, she restored and refreshed the house, bringing it up to date in a way that looks as though nothing was ever changed. Working with architect Dennis Gibbens, she opened up the kitchen and remade the master bath but retained important details, such as the exterior eaves supported by skinny posts. The side garden was redone by landscape architect Judy Horton and a much needed pool, located in the boxed-in backyard, was hand-dug by Fletcher Pools.

Interior decorator and tastemaker Joe Nye helped Anderson incorporate her elegant collection of heirloom furniture and art from yesterday and today, giving the potentially stark interiors a warm and inviting feel.

RIGHT *The entrance to Gregory Ain's Beckman Residence.* FOLLOWING PAGES *The living room includes an early-nineteenth-century Chinese tilt-top table and two Chinese trunks once owned by the owner's grandmother, Gloria Swanson. The painting* Balls *is by Eric Ernest Johnson.*

LEFT *A Bertoia chair next to a Chippendale armchair.*
Over the IKEA Surfboard table, a self-portrait by Hollace
Colburn.
ABOVE *An overview of the living room.*

RIGHT *The music room, including a portrait by Hugo Ballin.*
BELOW *Over the French antique console, two Julius Shulman prints are displayed. The one on the left is the owner's childhood home, and on the right is the current house.*

ANDERSON HOUSE

RUSTIC CANYON, 1950
CRAIG ELLWOOD, ARCHITECT

HIDDEN BEHIND AN UNASSUMING aluminum-and-brick facade, Craig Ellwood's Anderson House personifies the ideal of California modernism, presenting sophisticated shelter that blends seamlessly with its surrounding landscape. An extended wall of glass opens the master bedroom, living room, and kitchen up to the canyon forest garden outside. An enclosed courtyard ties in the kitchen with the kids' rooms.

Tastefully restored and renovated by decorator Laura Baker of The Uplifters, Inc., and her husband, Steven, the house is appointed with a quality selection of Modern furniture and decorative arts. She replaced a redwood wall that extends outside the house, added a new kitchen, and replaced a large closet with a wall of bookcases—all in Douglas fir to go with the ceiling. Working with architect Davida Rochlin, Baker also designed a glass-walled art studio that echoes the house in an homage to Ellwood that the architect surely would have appreciated.

RIGHT *An art studio designed to echo the house.*
FOLLOWING PAGES *A view of the house from the back. There are no windows facing the street.*

LEFT *In the open living room. Around the T. H. Robsjohn-Gibbings coffee table, a Stickley armchair,
Paul McCobb wing chairs, and a custom couch designed by Laura Baker.*
ABOVE *In the entry hall, a wall of closets were replaced by bookcases.* BELOW *The kitchen.*

ABOVE *A view through the children's room into the enclosed courtyard. The brick is painted white to the glass and continues outside unpainted.*
RIGHT *A view from the master bedroom.*
FOLLOWING PAGES *Looking out toward an old sycamore tree. Vintage rattan chair by Franco Albini and a Lightolier lamp. The owners replaced a dark redwood wall with a medium-tone Douglas fir that extends outside.*

MORGAN HOUSE

HANCOCK PARK, 1917
IRVING GILL, ARCHITECT

ARCHITECT IRVING GILL'S ARCHES are not an ode to the missions of El Camino Real but rather an homage to concrete and its potential as a modern material. Gill was a true Modern architect of his day, and his genius was touted by peers and fellow Adolf Loos students Richard Neutra and Rudolf Schindler. It is not hard to imagine that the simple pure architecture of the missions provided the young architect with inspiration. His plan for the San Diego Panama–California Exposition offered the potential to bridge the era's dual desires to wed the romanticized past with the promise of the future, but it was quashed in favor of a more ornamental revivalist theme. His experiments translated the Modern to the Mediterranean in a seamless manner and are a standing reminder of what could have become a defining template for greater Southern California.

The Morgan House, built in 1917, was one of a series of designs meant as prototypes intended for high-quality affordable single-family housing. It is a beautiful example of his work, constructed from poured-in-place concrete with carefully placed windows that paint the interior of the house with light and shadow throughout the day. It was carefully restored by artist and designer Roy McMakin and Andie Zelino. The stewards of the house have added a sympathetic guest studio and outdoor dining area and through and through have kept the whole well maintained.

RIGHT *The arched entryway to the house is at once bold and romantic.* FOLLOWING PAGES *The living room, with a Batchelder-tile fireplace. The painting at center,* Playing the Video, *is by Adam Shaw.*

ABOVE *The dining room with table and chairs designed by the former owner, artist Roy McMakin.*
RIGHT *Another view of the living room. The light is what makes Morgan House so special. There are clerestory windows and skylights throughout the house.*

LEFT *The back of the fireplace juts into the kitchen.*
RIGHT *The master bathroom, where photographer Dewey Nicks took advantage of the great light and shot many of his portraits.*

LEFT *The courtyard with a McMakin daybed.*
ABOVE *The bedroom.*

LEFT *The exterior hardscape, the bench, pond, and fire pit, as well as the Casita, were designed by the owner and built during an extensive renovation in 2006 after a careful study of Gill's body of work. The bench hides a barbecue behind it.*

A C K N O W L E D G M E N T S

WE WISH TO THANK our amazing publisher, Charles Miers, for his continued encouragement and support. Much gratitude goes to David Morton for his friendship and guidance and to Douglas Curran for being not just a great editor and friend but a spot-on designer to boot. And our sincere thanks to all of those who opened their homes to us or in other ways helped us on our way, including:

Brooke Anderson
Laura and Steven Baker
Jennifer and Joe Brooke
Mark Brooks
Pamela Burton and Richard Hertz
Althea Edwards
Mary Effron
Marie Gauthier
Lynn Hansen
Johnson Hartig
Tobey Horn and Harold Tomin
Paul Hunter
Whitney and Lee Kaplan
Mary Kennedy and Richard Keit
Hugh Levick
Frank Magallanes
Jeffrey McCall and David Wills
Jacqueline and John Millei
David and Elizabeth Netto
Sheharazad and Ron Fleming
Bill Podley

Carolyn Schnieder
Joel Shukovsky
Boyd Smith
Kathy Solomon and Bob Burchman
Meg Sullivan
Alisa Tager and David Pagel
Dayna and Bryan Ray Turcotte
Cristi Walden
Allegra, Lauren, and Christopher Woods
Caitlin Wylde
Diane Wilk and Michael Burch
Margaret -Yen and Eric Ernest Johnson
Victoria Yust and Ian McIlvaine
Sandrine and Alexander Yust

And our talented friend Joe Nye, whose style and enthusiasm will be greatly missed.